Words for Blessing the World

Poems in Hebrew and English

מִלִים לְבָרֵךְ אֶת הָעוֹלָם
שִׁירִים בְּעִבְרִית וּבְאַנְגְלִית

Herbert J. Levine

Ben Yehuda Press
Teaneck, New Jersey

WORDS FOR BLESSING THE WORLD ©2017 Herbert J. Levine. All rights reserved. No part of this book may be used or reproduced in any manner whatsoever without written permission except in the case of brief quotations embodied in critical articles and reviews.

Published by Ben Yehuda Press
122 Ayers Court #1B
Teaneck, NJ 07666

http://www.BenYehudaPress.com

Jewish Poetry Project #5
http://jpoetry.us

To subscribe to our monthly book club and support independent Jewish publishing, visit https://www.patreon.com/BenYehudaPress

ISBN13 978-1-934730-64-5

19 20 21 / 10 9 8 7 6 5 4   20191222

Dedication

To my brother, Steven –– לאחי שלמה זלמן
in solidarity

Acknowledgements

The teacher from whom I first learned to live inside Hebrew poetry was Anne Lapidus Lerner. I am delighted that she has the chance to see how her teachings live on in me. In a similar vein, I am grateful for Marcia Falk's *The Book of Blessings* and *The Days Between*, which showed me that an American Jewish poet writing poems in Hebrew could have the ambition to push Jewish civilization forward in new ways.

As a non-native speaker of Hebrew, I benefited from the encouragement and expertise of others. I want to thank my friends Ori Alon, Hanoch Guy, Adina Newberg and Reena Spicehandler for their generous reading and critiques of my work in my second language. I am especially indebted to Hanoch Guy, who read my poems with the ear and eye of a poet. While I appreciate all the suggestions that I received, responsibility for the final versions is mine.

I am pleased to acknowledge the journals and website that previously published parts of this book. "Blessed Are You, World," in its present bi-lingual form, appeared in *Jewish Currents* (Summer, 2017). Three of the English-language poems in this collection were previously published in slightly different form. A prose version of Part 1 of "All in the Family" was published as part of "Family Plot" in *Jewish Literary Journal* (Feb. 2015). The entire English version of "All in the Family" had its first appearance on the Shalom Center website: theshalomcenter.org/content/occupation-50-now-what-jubilee. Part 4 of "Bible Lost and Found" was published in *Tikkun*, v. 7,6 (1992) as "Esau's Curse." "To Yehuda Amichai" was published in *Tikkun* v. 25, 5 (2010). A longer version of the Author's Afterword appeared in *Tikkun* v. 32,1 (Winter, 2017).

Table of Contents

I

Blessed Are You, World	2
Don't Think There's No More Prayer	8
Meditations on the Names of God	14

II

This is the Torah	20
All in the Family	22
Bible, Lost and Found	26
I Believe with Perfect Faith	34

III

As Our Father Neared Death	38
To Yehuda Amichai	40
What I Received as an Inheritance	42
I Make a Covenant of Peace with You	44

IV

Rebbe Nachman's Torah of the Void	48
Song for Gratitude	50

Author's Afterword	53

תֹּכֶן הַשִּׁירִים

I

3   בָּרוּךְ אַתָּה עוֹלָם
9   אַל תַּחֲשֹׁב שֶׁאֵין תְּפִילָה
15 הִרְהוּרִים עַל שְׁמוֹת הַשֵּׁם

II

21 זֹאת הַתּוֹרָה
23 הַכֹּל בַּמִּשְׁפָּחָה
27 תַּנַ"ךְ, אָבוּד וְנִמְצָא
35 אֲנִי מַאֲמִין בֶּאֱמוּנָה שְׁלֵמָה

III

39 כְּשֶׁאָבִינוּ גָּסַס
41 לִיהוּדָה עֲמִיחַי
43 מַה שֶׁקִּבַּלְתִּי בִּירוּשָׁה
45 אֲנִי כּוֹרֶת בְּרִית עִמְּךָ

IV

49 תּוֹרַת הֶחָלָל לְרַבִּי נַחְמָן
51 שִׁיר לְהוֹדָיָה

53 סוֹף דָּבָר

I

Blessed Are You, World

1.
In the archives of Kibbutz Beit-HaShita,
I discovered forgotten hand-written notes
for a Passover Seder from 1927.
Instead of the Kiddush, the author wrote,
"Blessed are you, kibbutz."
In his footsteps, I widen the blessing circle
and say, blessed are you, world —
to praise your fragile, complex beauty.

2.
If you call the earth your mother who birthed you in pain
from the wombs of the mothers from Eve until now,
if you call the world your friend who upholds
you, whether in a day of trouble or of joy,
if you call the universe your help-meet,
who gives strength to both your weakness and your might,
then join with me in these songs
and we'll sing together in a world
that fills our springs with blessings.

Herbert Levine

בָּרוּךְ אַתָּה עוֹלָם

1

בָּאַרְכִיוֹן קִבּוּץ בֵּית הַשִּׁטָּה
גִּילִיתִי כְּתַב־יַד נִשְׁכָּח
לְסֵדֶר לֵיל פֶּסַח מִשְּׁנַת 1927.
בִּמְקוֹם הַקִּידוּשׁ הַמְחַבֵּר כָּתַב,
בָּרוּךְ אַתָּה קִבּוּץ.
בְּעִקְבוֹתָיו, אֲנִי מַרְחִיב אֶת מַעֲגַל
הַבְּרָכָה וְאוֹמֵר, בָּרוּךְ אַתָּה עוֹלָם —
לְשַׁבֵּחַ אֶת יָפְיְךָ הָעֲדִין וְהַמֻּרְכָּב.

2

אִם תִּקְרְאִי לָאֲדָמָה אֵם שֶׁהוֹלִידָה אוֹתָךְ בְּעֶצֶב
מֵרַחֲמֵי הָאִמָּהוֹת מֵחַוָּה עַד עַכְשָׁיו,
אִם תִּקְרָא לָעוֹלָם חָבֵר שֶׁתּוֹמֵךְ בְּךָ
בְּיוֹם צָרָה אוֹ בְּיוֹם שִׂמְחָה,
אִם תִּקְרְאִי לַיְקוּם עֵזֶר כְּנֶגְדֵּךְ
הַנּוֹתֵן כֹּחַ לְחֻלְשָׁתֵךְ וְגַם לְעַצְמָתֵךְ,
אָז תִּצְטָרֵף אֵלַי בְּשִׁירִים אֵלֶּה
וְנָשִׁירָה יַחַד בָּעוֹלָם
שֶׁמְּמַלֵּא מַעְיָנוֹתֵינוּ בְּרָכוֹת.

3.
Planet orbiting the sun from time's beginning
till its end, planet, blue, green and white,
planet, covered with water and land and sky,
planet made of forests, lakes and seas, fields and sandy beaches,
Planet Earth that we have seen from space
complete and alive before our astonished eyes!

4.
When I ask my friend how he's doing,
he answers me, 'Thank God,'
and he would respond thus even
if he were suffering great distress.
I think, but don't respond to him:
Thanks, earth, from which I came
at my birth; during my life
I have grown a sensitive soul,
but I will return to the earth at my death
without a soul and without pain,
thanks to the embrace of the earth.

5.
Like the enthusiastic kibbutznik
who insisted on making his time new,
let us make new what's old and make holy what's new
and join what's called secular to what's called holy
and what's called material to what's called spiritual
until the gulf between them disappears.

3

כַּדּוּר סוֹבֵב אֶת הַשֶּׁמֶשׁ מִתְּחִלַּת הַזְּמַן
עַד סוֹפוֹ, כַּדּוּר כָּחֹל, יָרֹק וְלָבָן,
כַּדּוּר כְּסוּי מַיִם, אֲדָמָה וְשָׁמַיִם,
כַּדּוּר עָשׂוּי יְעָרוֹת, אֲגַמִּים וְיַמִּים, שָׂדוֹת וְחוֹלוֹת,
כַּדּוּר הָאָרֶץ שֶׁרָאִינוּ אוֹתוֹ מֵהֶחָלָל
שָׁלֵם וְחַי לִפְנֵי עֵינֵינוּ הַנִּדְהָמוֹת!

4.

כְּשֶׁאֲנִי שׁוֹאֵל לִשְׁלוֹם חֲבֵרִי
הוּא עוֹנֶה לִי, תּוֹדָה לָאֵל,
וְהָיָה עוֹנֶה כָּכָה אֲפִלּוּ
אִם הוּא סוֹבֵל יִסּוּרִים קָשִׁים.
אֲנִי חוֹשֵׁב וְלֹא עוֹנֶה לוֹ,
תּוֹדָה לָאֲדָמָה שֶׁיָּצָאתִי מִמֶּנָּה
בְּהִוָּלְדִי; מֶשֶׁךְ חַיַּי
טִפַּחְתִּי נְשָׁמָה רְגִישָׁה,
אֲבָל אָשׁוּב לָאֲדָמָה בְּמוֹתִי
בְּלִי נְשָׁמָה וּבְלִי יִסּוּרִים,
בִּזְכוּת חִבּוּק הָאֲדָמָה.

5.

כְּמוֹ הַקִּבּוּצְנִיק הַמִּתְלַהֵב
שֶׁהִתְעַקֵּשׁ לְחַדֵּשׁ אֶת יָמָיו,
נְחַדֵּשׁ אֶת הַיָּשָׁן וּנְקַדֵּשׁ אֶת הֶחָדָשׁ
וּנְחַבֵּר מַה שֶּׁנִּקְרָא חִלּוֹנִי לְמַה שֶּׁנִּקְרָא קָדוֹשׁ
וּמַה שֶּׁנִּקְרָא גַּשְׁמִי לְמַה שֶּׁנִּקְרָא רוּחָנִי
עַד שֶׁהַתְּהוֹם בֵּינֵיהֶם יֵעָלֵם.

6.
They say that our life began through a crack
in the ocean floor, through which heat rose
and still rises from the molten core of the earth
and catalyzed the salty waters, giving birth
to the amino acids, in them the history of life
in the sea, on land and in the air.
The psalmist sings, "with you is the source of life."
Every day, I too acknowledge the source of life
that still enlivens my breath.

7.
From Einstein and his students I learned
that the elements in me were forged
in the same furnace as the stars.
From other great ones, I've learned
to sit, breathe, pay attention
with watchful eyes
to a world filled with glory and wonders
like me, like you and like the stars.

8.
O blessed world, you give us each day
visions and problems to solve and to praise.

6.

אוֹמְרִים שֶׁחַיֵּינוּ הִתְחִילוּ דֶּרֶךְ סֶדֶק
בְּקַרְקָעִית הָאוֹקְיָינוּס; מִמֶּנּוּ עָלָה חֹם,
וַעֲדַיִין עוֹלֶה, מִתּוֹכוֹ הַמֻּתָּךְ שֶׁל כַּדּוּר הָאָרֶץ
וְזֵרֵז אֶת הַמַּיִם הַמְּלוּחִים. כָּךְ נִבְרְאוּ
הַחֻמְצוֹת הָאֲמִינִיּוֹת וּבָהֶן תּוֹלְדוֹת הַחַיִּים
בְּתוֹךְ יַמִּים, עַל אֲדָמוֹת וּבָאֲוִיר.
שָׁר הַמְזַמֵּר, 'עִמְּךָ מְקוֹר חַיִּים.'
גַּם אֲנִי מוֹדֶה בְּכָל יוֹם לִמְקוֹר הַחַיִּים
שֶׁעֲדַיִין מְחַיֶּה אֶת הַנְּשִׁימָה בְּקִרְבִּי.

7.

מֵאַיְנְשְׁטַיְין וְתַלְמִידָיו לָמַדְתִּי
שֶׁהָאֶלֶמֶנְטִים שֶׁבְּקִרְבִּי נִתְעַצְּבוּ
בְּאוֹתוֹ הַתַּנּוּר שֶׁבּוֹ נִדְלְקוּ הַכּוֹכָבִים.
מִגְּדוֹלִים אֲחֵרִים לָמַדְתִּי
לָשֶׁבֶת, לִנְשֹׁם, לְהַקְשִׁיב
בְּעֵינַיִים פְּקוּחוֹת
לְעוֹלָם מָלֵא הָדָר וְנִפְלָאוֹת
כָּמוֹנִי, כָּמוֹךְ וּכְמוֹ הַכּוֹכָבִים.

8.

בָּרוּךְ אַתָּה עוֹלָם שֶׁנּוֹתֵן לָנוּ בְּכָל יוֹם
דְּמֻיּוֹת וּבְעָיוֹת לִפְתּוֹר וּלְשַׁבֵּחַ.

Don't Think There Is No Prayer

1.
Don't think there is no prayer
in a world without a master;
in Hebrew, to pray is a reflexive verb.
You need only yourself —
the 'I' that fears, makes people mad, and complains,
and the 'I' that includes
all the 'I's in the world,
and asks that you have compassion on yourself
and on them all.

2.
Just as the lad Abram put a hammer
in the hand of the biggest idol
in his father's workshop
and pointed to it as the one who shattered
all the rest, so our father Abraham
put that self-same hammer in our hands
so that we might destroy images of God
which, since then, have screened us from seeing
that there is nothing holier than the world.

3.
Everyone carries a sack on his or her shoulder,
full of the emotional wounds
that one suffers during his or her life,
but those who are healthy seek to lighten
the load of memories.

אַל תַּחְשׁב שֶׁאֵין תְּפִילָה

1.

אַל תַּחְשׁב שֶׁאֵין תְּפִילָה
בְּעוֹלָם שֶׁאֵין בּוֹ אָדוֹן;
לְהִתְפַּלֵּל זֶה בִּנְיָן הִתְפַּעֵל.
אַתָּה זָקוּק רַק לְעַצְמְךָ —
הָאֲנִי שֶׁמְּפַחֵד וּמַרְגִּיז וּמִתְלוֹנֵן,
וְהָאָנוֹכִי שֶׁכּוֹלֵל
אֶת כָּל הָאֲנִיִּים שֶׁבָּעוֹלָם
וְדוֹרֵשׁ מִמְּךָ לְרַחֵם עַל עַצְמְךָ
וְעַל כֻּלָּם.

2.

כְּמוֹ שֶׁהַנַּעַר אַבְרָם שָׂם פַּטִּישׁ
בְּיַד הָאֱלִיל הֲכִי־גָּדוֹל
בְּבֵית מְלֶאכֶת אָבִיו
וְהִצְבִּיעַ עָלָיו שֶׁשִּׁבֵּר אֶת יֶתֶר
הָאֱלִילִים, כָּךְ אַבְרָהָם אָבִינוּ
שָׂם אוֹתוֹ הַפַּטִּישׁ בְּיָדֵינוּ
כְּדֵי שֶׁנְּשַׁבֵּר אֶת דְּמֻיּוֹת הָאֱלֹהִים
שֶׁמֵּאָז מָסְכוּ אוֹתָנוּ מִלִּרְאוֹת
שֶׁאֵין קָדוֹשׁ כָּעוֹלָם.

3.

כָּל אֶחָד נוֹשֵׂא שַׂק עַל שִׁכְמוֹ אוֹ שִׁכְמָהּ,
מָלֵא כָּל הַנְּגָעִים הָרִגְשִׁיִּים
שֶׁסָּבְלוּ מֶשֶׁךְ חַיָּיו אוֹ חַיֶּיהָ
וְהַבְּרִיאִים מְבַקְשִׁים לְהָקֵל
אֶת עֹל הַזִּכְרוֹנוֹת.

Words for Blessing the World

The Jewish God also carries
a giant sack on His shoulders and is bent over
by the weighty disappointments of the Jews
that He did not honor his promises to them.
He too wants to be healthy,
so he prays to his children:
"The burden of your hopes and disappointments
is too heavy for me to bear. Please,
my children, let me put down my sack;
stop believing in me."

4.
Every Rosh Hashanah during my childhood, my father
would ask my Bubbe, "why are the corners
of your prayer book's pages folded over?"
Every year she answered him, "This is where we cry."
From her life of wandering
my Bubbe understood tears
and their consequences: in no way
challenge fate by failing to mention
the One who watches over all,
but hope with 'the help of God' and be
grateful with 'Praise God,' and 'Thank God.'
I also want to express hopes and
give thanks for the good in my life
and be amazed by the wonders of the universe.
With the help of the world,
my tongue is getting used to new expressions.

גַּם הָאֱלֹהִים הַיְהוּדִי נוֹשֵׂא
שַׂק עָצוּם עַל שִׁכְמוֹ וְהוּא כָּפוּף
מִכֹּבֶד הָאַכְזָבוֹת שֶׁל הַיְהוּדִים
שֶׁאֱלֹהֵיהֶם לֹא קִיֵּם אֶת הַבְטָחוֹתָיו.
גַּם הוּא רוֹצֶה לִהְיוֹת בָּרִיא,
לָכֵן הוּא מִתְפַּלֵּל לִפְנֵי בָּנָיו:
'עֹמֶס הַתִּקְוָה וְהָאַכְזָבָה
שֶׁלָּכֶם כָּבֵד לִי מִנְּשֹׂא. בְּבַקָּשָׁה,
יְלָדַי, תְּנוּ לִי לְהוֹרִיד אֶת שַׂקִּי;
אַל תּוֹסִיפוּ לְהַאֲמִין בִּי.'

4.

כָּל רֹאשׁ הַשָּׁנָה בְּיַלְדוּתִי, אָבִי הָיָה
שׁוֹאֵל אֶת סַבְתָּא, 'לָמָה פִּינוֹת
הַדַּפִּים בְּמַחְזוֹרֵךְ מְקֻפָּלוֹת?'
בְּכָל שָׁנָה עָנְתָה לוֹ, 'פֹּה בּוֹכִים.'
מֵחַיֶּיהָ מְלֵאֵי נְדוּדִים
סַבְתָּא הֵבִינָה הֵיטֵב אֶת הַדְּמָעוֹת
וְתוֹלְדוֹתֵיהֶן: אֵין דֶּרֶךְ
לְהִתְגָּרוֹת בַּגּוֹרָל מִבְּלִי לְהַזְכִּיר
אֶת זֶה שֶׁמַּשְׁגִּיחַ עַל הַכֹּל,
אֶלָּא לְקַוּוֹת בְּעֶזְרַת הַשֵּׁם וּלְהַכִּיר
אֶת הַטּוֹב בְּבָרוּךְ הַשֵּׁם וְתוֹדָה לָאֵל.
גַּם אֲנִי רוֹצָה לְהַבִּיעַ תִּקְווֹת,
לְהוֹדוֹת עַל הַטּוֹב שֶׁבְּחַיַּי
וְלִהְיוֹת מוּפְתַּע מִפִּלְאֵי הַיְקוּם.
בְּעֶזְרַת הָעוֹלָם,
לְשׁוֹנִי מִתְרַגֶּלֶת לְבִטּוּיִים חֲדָשִׁים.

5.
This is my prayer and my path in life:
to betroth the world in its fullness,
to serve others in joy,
to act towards them in love and truth,
to trust that right living and peace will bloom.

5.
זֹאת תְּפִילָתִי וְדֶרֶךְ חַיַּי:
לְהִתְאָרֵס עִם הָעוֹלָם הַמָּלֵא,
לַעֲבֹד אֲחֵרִים בְּשִׂמְחָה,
לְהִתְנַהֵג עִמָּם בְּחֶסֶד וּבֶאֱמֶת,
וְלִבְטֹחַ שֶׁצֶּדֶק וְשָׁלוֹם יִפְרָחוּ.

Meditations on the Names of God

1.
We must praise human imagination
for fashioning God in the image of the human
and calling God one and singular to get us used
to the unity of the world
and all that live in it.

2.
When Moses hesitated to accept his mission as messenger
to the children of Israel, God said to him,
"Tell them that Ehyeh —I will be— sent me to you,"
thereby revealing God's secret name,
I will be what I will be, meaning, "you will not
grasp the arc of the world in any
name or form. My purpose will be known
by what you become in the future;
If you stand up for what's right and are kind,
you'll reveal that the name, 'I will be'
will set you free from the rule of my name."

3.
Our world is a giant emergency room
where everyone gets a turn.
Until then, we care for those who are waiting in line:
the father who hugs his son who suffers silently,
the mother who names for her daughters the fear
of violence that women endure,
the neighbor who pays attention to the complaint

הִרְהוּרִים עַל שְׁמוֹת הַשֵּׁם

1.

עָלֵינוּ לְשַׁבֵּחַ אֶת דִּמְיוֹן הָאָדָם
שֶׁיָּצַר אֶת הַבּוֹרֵא בִּדְמוּת הָאָדָם
וּקְרָאוֹ אֶחָד וְיָחִיד לְהַרְגִּילֵנוּ
לְאַחְדוּת הָעוֹלָם
וְכָל הַנְּפָשׁוֹת הַחַיּוֹת.

2.

כְּשֶׁמֹשֶׁה הִסֵּס לְקַבֵּל תַּפְקִידוֹ כְּשָׁלִיחַ
לִבְנֵי יִשְׂרָאֵל, הָאֱלֹהִים אָמַר לוֹ,
'תֹּאמַר לָהֶם שֶׁאֶהְיֶה שְׁלָחַנִי אֲלֵיכֶם,'
וְגִלָּה אֶת שְׁמוֹ הַסּוֹדִי,
אֶהְיֶה אֲשֶׁר אֶהְיֶה, וּמוּבָנוֹ, 'לֹא תָּבִינוּ
אֶת תַּכְלִית הָעוֹלָם בְּכָל
שֵׁם אוֹ צוּרָה. מַטָּרָתִי תִּגָּלֶה
דֶּרֶךְ מַה שֶּׁתִּהְיוּ בֶּעָתִיד;
אִם תִּתְמְכוּ בַּיֹּשֶׁר וְתִגְמְלוּ חֶסֶד אֶחָד לַשֵּׁנִי,
תְּגַלּוּ שֶׁהַשֵּׁם אֶהְיֶה
יְשַׁחְרֵר אֶתְכֶם מִשִּׁלְטוֹן שְׁמִי.'

3.

עוֹלָמֵנוּ חֶדֶר טִיפּוּל-נִמְרָץ עָצוּם
וּלְכָל אֶחָד תּוֹר.
בֵּינָתַיִם נִטָּפֵל בְּאֵלֶּה שֶׁמְּחַכִּים בַּתּוֹר:
הָאָב הַמְּחַבֵּק אֶת בְּנוֹ בְּצַעַר דּוֹמֵם,
הָאֵם הַקּוֹרֵאת בְּשֵׁם לִבְנוֹתֶיהָ
אֶת פַּחַד הָאֲלִימוּת שֶׁנָּשִׁים סוֹבְלוֹת,
הַשָּׁכֵן שֶׁמַּקְשִׁיב לִתְלוּנַת שְׁכֵנוֹ

Words for Blessing the World

of his neighbor against the city, and even though he has heard it
many times, listens once again with an open heart.
Rabbis say that we learn compassion
from the Compassionate One, but I say
that gods learn compassion
only from compassionate men and women,
whom I praise.

4.
Rabbis say that The Place is the place
of the world, but that the world is not His place,
and I say that the place of the world is indeed our place;
there is no other
and how awesome it is.

נֶגֶד הָעִירִיָּה, וְאֲפִילוּ שֶׁשְּׁמָעוֹ
פְּעָמִים רַבּוֹת, שׁוֹמֵעַ שׁוּב בְּטוּב לֵב.
רַבָּנִים אוֹמְרִים שֶׁאָנוּ לוֹמְדִים רַחֲמָנוּת
מֵהַנְהָגָתוֹ שֶׁל הָרַחֲמָן, אֲבָל אֲנִי אוֹמֵר
שֶׁאֱלֹהִים לוֹמְדִים רַחֲמָנוּת
מֵהָרַחֲמָנִיִּים וְהָרַחֲמָנִיּוֹת,
שֶׁאוֹתָם אֲנִי מְשַׁבֵּחַ.

4.

רַבָּנִים אוֹמְרִים שֶׁהַמָּקוֹם הוּא מְקוֹמוֹ
שֶׁל הָעוֹלָם וְשֶׁהָעוֹלָם אֵינוֹ מְקוֹמוֹ,
וְאֲנִי אוֹמֵר שֶׁמְּקוֹם הָעוֹלָם הוּא כֵן מְקוֹמֵנוּ;
אֵין עוֹד מִלְבַדּוֹ
וּמַה נּוֹרָא הַמָּקוֹם הַזֶּה.

Herbert Levine

II

This is the Torah

This is the Torah
that was written by human beings
over many generations
that Ezra put before the people of Israel
in the name of Moses
that Hillel the elder summarized
hundreds of years after Ezra:
What is hateful to you, don't do to your fellow.
The rest is commentary that's worth studying
and, afterwards, do what needs doing.

Our ancestors were right when they said that one mitzvah
leads to another and, likewise, a misdeed.
This I know from the mistakes of my life.
I don't believe in a commander, but the language of
"Thou shalt" reminds me that we inherited
the mitzvot in order to be refined,
like silver in the hands of the smith,
like gold separated from its dross.

זֹאת הַתּוֹרָה

זֹאת הַתּוֹרָה
שֶׁנִּכְתְּבָה עַל יְדֵי בְּנֵי אָדָם
מֶשֶׁךְ דּוֹרוֹת דּוֹרוֹת,
שֶׁשָּׂם עֶזְרָא לִפְנֵי בְּנֵי יִשְׂרָאֵל
בְּשֵׁם מֹשֶׁה,
שֶׁסִּכֵּם הַזָּקֵן הִלֵּל
מֵאוֹת שָׁנִים אַחֲרֵי עֶזְרָא:
מַה שֶּׁשָּׂנוּא עָלֶיךָ אַל תַּעֲשֶׂה לַחֲבֵרְךָ
וְהַיֶּתֶר פֵּרוּשׁ שֶׁכְּדַאי לִלְמוֹד
וְאַחַר כָּךְ תַּעֲשֶׂה מַה שֶּׁצָּרִיךְ.

אֲבוֹתֵינוּ צָדְקוּ כְּשֶׁאָמְרוּ שֶׁמִּצְוָה
גּוֹרֶרֶת מִצְוָה וַעֲבֵרָה, עֲבֵרָה.
אֶת זֶה אֲנִי יוֹדֵעַ מִשְּׁגִיאוֹת חַיַּי
אֵינִי מַאֲמִין בְּמִצְוָה, אֲבָל לְשׁוֹן
צִוּוּי מַזְכִּירָה לִי שֶׁהַמִּצְווֹת
נִמְסְרוּ לְיָדֵינוּ לְצָרְפֵנוּ,
כְּכֶסֶף בְּיַד הַצּוֹרֵף,
כְּזָהָב נִבְדָּל מִבְּדִילוֹ.

All in the Family

1.
We sat, my brother and I, in the back
of the family car and quarreled unceasingly
until our mother, may she rest in peace, would ask,
'How will there be peace in the world if two brothers cannot
live together in peace?' We knew
from the Torah stories she had taught us
that Cain killed his brother Hevel out of jealousy,
that Jacob was ready to steal and Esau
to murder to receive what he could never get,
the one, indivisible blessing.
Nowadays my brother and I meet for meals
on our birthdays, talk of our cholesterol levels
and sleep apnea, of the jobs that the kids
have taken, and of the Israelis and Palestinians,
he, embarrassed, like a Diaspora Jew, and I, shaken
by this quarrel of brothers who rise from their graves like ghosts
to deceive and to fight, to die and to kill, united only
by their family plot, where they
pause for a moment to bury their dead.

2.
The Palestinians commemorate their tragic Naqba,
a holy day of remembering and mourning the loss
of their nation. When the day comes that they celebrate
the beginning of their state, I suggest they also celebrate
a Palestinian Purim, with costumes, masks and hashish
(the Muslims won't be drinking alcohol),

הַכֹּל בַּמִּשְׁפָּחָה

1.

יָשַׁבְנוּ, אֲנִי וְאָחִי, בַּמּוֹשָׁב הָאֲחוֹרִי
בִּמְכוֹנִית הַמִּשְׁפָּחָה וְרַבְנוּ בְּלִי הֶפְסֵק
עַד שֶׁאִמֵּנוּ, עָלֶיהָ הַשָּׁלוֹם, הָיְתָה שׁוֹאֶלֶת,
'אֵיךְ יָבֹא שָׁלוֹם בָּעוֹלָם אִם שְׁנֵי אַחִים אֵינָם
יְכוֹלִים לִחְיוֹת בְּשַׁלְוָה?' יָדַעְנוּ
מִסִּפּוּרֵי תּוֹרָה שֶׁהִיא לִמְּדָה אוֹתָנוּ
שֶׁקַּיִן הָרַג אֶת הֶבֶל אָחִיו מִקִּנְאָה,
שֶׁיַּעֲקֹב הָיָה מוּכָן לִגְנֹב וְעֵשָׂו
לִרְצֹחַ לְקַבֵּל מַה שֶׁאַף פַּעַם לֹא יְקַבֵּל,
הַבְּרָכָה הַיְחִידָה שֶׁלֹּא נִיתֶּנֶת לַחֲלוּקָה.
כָּעֵת אֲנִי וְאָחִי נִפְגָּשִׁים לִסְעוּדוֹת
יְמֵי הַלֶּדֶת, מְדַבְּרִים עַל רָמוֹת הַכִּילֶסְטְרוֹל
וְעַל דֹּם הַנְּשִׁימָה בַּשֵּׁינָה, עַל הַמִּשְׂרוֹת שֶׁקִּבְּלוּ
הַיְלָדִים וְעַל הַיִּשְׂרְאֵלִים וְהַפָלֶסְטִינָאִים,
הוּא נָבוֹךְ כִּיהוּדִי מֵהַגּוֹלָה וַאֲנִי רוֹעֵד
מֵרִיב הָאַחִים שֶׁקָּמִים מִקִּבְרֵיהֶם כִּרְפָאִים
לִרְמוֹת וּלְהִלָּחֵם, לָמוּת וּלְהָמִית, מְאֻחָדִים רַק
בְּקֶבֶר הַמִּשְׁפַּחְתִּי שֶׁלָּהֶם,
שֶׁשּׂוֹהִים שָׁם לְרֶגַע לִקְבֹּר אֶת מֵתֵיהֶם

2.

הַפָלֶסְטִינָאִים חוֹגְגִים הַנַּכְּבָּא הַטְרָגִי שֶׁלָּהֶם
עֲצֶרֶת קְדוֹשָׁה לִזְכֹּר וּלְהִתְאַבֵּל עַל אוֹבְדַן
עַמָּם. יָבֹא יוֹם וְיָחֹגּוּ אֶת תְּחִילַת מְדִינָתָם,
אֲנִי מַצִּיעַ שֶׁיָּחֹגּוּ גַּם,
חַג פּוּרִים פַלֶסְטִינַאִי עִם תִּלְבָּשׁוֹת, מַסֵּכוֹת וְחָשִׁישׁ
(הַמּוּסְלְמִים לֹא יִשְׁתּוּ יִ"שׁ)

when they'll wipe out the name of Israel
once a year, and they'll say what Jews say
on Hanukah, Passover and Purim: They tried to kill us
but they failed, so let's eat rich food
and tell funny stories
to keep living well and not fall
to the bottom of memory's black hole
of tears and shame and fury.

3.
Let's be like dreamers again. In days to come,
let's say in forty more years,
when the Israelis and Palestinians declare
their mutual state,
they will look back and see its start in their decision
to teach their children both Arabic and Hebrew,
for in the supple and sinuous letters, they saw
the face of the one land that they both love.

וְיִמְחוּ אֶת הַשֵּׁם יִשְׂרָאֵל פַּעַם בְּשָׁנָה
וְיֹאמְרוּ מַה שֶׁיְּהוּדִים אוֹמְרִים
בְּחֲנוּכָּה, בְּפּוּרִים וּבְפֶּסַח: הִשְׁתַּדְּלוּ לְהָרְגֵנוּ
וְנִכְשְׁלוּ; בֹּאוּ וְנֹאכַל אוֹכֶל מְצֻיָּן
וּנְסַפֵּר סִפּוּרִים מַצְחִיקִים
לְהַמְשִׁיךְ לִחְיוֹת חַיִּים טוֹבִים וְשֶׁלֹּא נֵרֵד
לְתַחְתִּית הַזִּכָּרוֹן, בּוֹר שָׁחוֹר
שֶׁל דְּמָעוֹת, בּוּשָׁה וְחֵמָה.

3.
נִהְיֶה שׁוּב כְּחוֹלְמִים. בַּיָּמִים הַבָּאִים,
נֹאמַר בְּעוֹד אַרְבָּעִים שָׁנִים,
כְּשֶׁיַּכְרִיזוּ הַיִּשְׂרְאֵלִים וְהַפַּלֶשְׂתִּינִים
מְדִינָתָם הַמְשֻׁתֶּפֶת
יִסְתַּכְּלוּ אֲחוֹרַנִּית וְיִרְאוּ הַתְחָלָתָהּ בַּהַחְלָטָה
לְלַמֵּד לִבְנֵיהֶם גַּם עֲרָבִית גַּם עִבְרִית,
כִּי בְּאוֹתִיּוֹת, גְּמִישׁוֹת וּמְפֻתָּלוֹת, רָאוּ
פְּנֵי הָאָרֶץ הַיְּחִידָה שֶׁשְּׁנֵיהֶם אוֹהֲבִים.

Bible, Lost and Found

1.
I was once at a meeting of a religious kibbutz
and heard a debate between two of the movement's big men,
one pointing his finger at the Bible as proof for the boundaries
of Greater Israel and the other striking
the book and announcing: One does not learn
to live from this book! And I add that
in our days it is urgent that we learn
from what is not written in the Bible ––
from the white spaces
between the black words.

2.
Why do you walk bent over, Cain,
so you can't see anyone's face?
"In every face, I see the face of my brother, Hevel.
Everything is hevel — nothingness."

3.
Why do you walk backwards, Ham,
without seeing the way in front of you?
"I see nothing except a vision of my father's privates.
Will it disappear if I walk forward?"

תַּנַ״ךְ אָבוּד וְנִמְצָא

1.

פַּעַם הָיִיתִי בַּאֲסֵיפַת קִיבּוּץ דָּתִי
וְשָׁמַעְתִּי וִיכּוּחַ בֵּין שְׁנֵי גְדוֹלֵי הַתְּנוּעָה,
אֶחָד מַצְבִּיעַ עַל הַתַּנַ״ךְ כְּהוֹכָחָה לִגְבוּלוֹת
אֶרֶץ יִשְׂרָאֵל הַשְּׁלֵמָה וְהַשֵּׁנִי מַכֶּה
בַּסֵּפֶר וּמַכְרִיז: אֵין לוֹמְדִים
לִחְיוֹת מֵהַסֵּפֶר הַזֶּה! וַאֲנִי מוֹסִיף
שֶׁבְּיָמֵינוּ דָחוּף לִלְמֹד
מִמַּה שֶׁלֹּא כָּתוּב בַּתַּנַ״ךְ —
בַּחֲלָלִים הַלְּבָנִים
בֵּין הַתֵּבוֹת הַשְּׁחוֹרוֹת.

2.

לָמָה תֵלֵךְ כָּפוּף, קַיִן,
וְלֹא תוּכַל לִרְאוֹת פְּנֵי אִישׁ?
'בְּכָל פָּנִים אֲנִי רוֹאֶה אֶת פְּנֵי הֶבֶל אָחִי.
הַכֹּל הֶבֶל.'

3.

לָמָה תִּפְנֶה אֲחוֹרָה, חָם,
בְּלִי לִרְאוֹת אֶת הַדֶּרֶךְ לְפָנֶיךָ?
'אֵינִי רוֹאֶה דָּבָר חוּץ מִמַּרְאֵה מְבוּשֵׁי אָבִי.
הַאִם יֵעָלֵם אִם אֶפְנֶה קָדִימָה?'

Words for Blessing the World

4.
Why is your mouth open, Dinah,
and no voice heard?
"My brothers raped me, blamed another and murdered him
and till today my story has not been told."

5.
Why do you sit in the corner, Tamar, royal daughter,
without shoes and with your clothes all torn?
"My brother tore my clothes, taking me as his whore.
Women like me don't go outside."

6.
"Of course you hated your father all these years.
Who wouldn't hate him after he threw us out?
But we lived and our family has done well.
There's no spice trade like yours in all Arabia.
You are his first-born, Ishmael.
Why should Sarah's son inherit his wealth and honor?
You have twelve sons to his two.
Take your sons to Hebron and bury your father.
Stand next to the grave before her son
and claim what's yours."

7.
"They convinced me to marry a woman from our kin—
I knew that they despised my Canaanite wives,
so I swore that I wouldn't marry another local girl.
I crossed the Yabbok,
met with Uncle Ishmael,

4.

לָמָה פִּיךְ פָּתוּחַ, דִּינָה,
וְקוֹלֵךְ לֹא נִשְׁמַע?
'אַחַי עִנּוּ אוֹתִי, הֶאֱשִׁימוּ אַחֵר וְרָצְחָהוּ
וְעַד הַיּוֹם סִיפּוּרִי אֵינוֹ מְסֻפָּר.'

5.

לָמָה אַתְּ יוֹשֶׁבֶת בַּפִּינָה, תָּמָר, בַּת מֶלֶךְ,
בְּלִי נַעֲלַיִם וּבִבְגָדִים קְרוּעִים?
'אָחִי קָרַע אֶת בִּגְדִי כְּשֶׁלָּקַח אוֹתִי כְּזוֹנָה.
נָשִׁים כָּמוֹנִי לֹא יוֹצְאוֹת הַחוּצָה.'

6.

'בְּוַדַּאי שֶׁשָּׂנֵאתָ אֶת אָבִיךְ מֶשֶׁךְ כָּל הַשָּׁנִים.
מִי לֹא יִשְׂנָא אוֹתוֹ אַחֲרֵי שֶׁגֵּרֵשׁ אוֹתָנוּ?
אֲבָל חָיִינוּ, וּמִשְׁפַּחְתֵּנוּ הִצְלִיחָה.
אֵין מִסְחַר תַּבְלִינִים כְּמוֹ שֶׁלְּךָ בְּכָל עֲרָב.
אַתָּה בְּכוֹרוֹ, יִשְׁמָעֵאל.
לָמָה הַבֵּן שֶׁל שָׂרָה יִירַשׁ אֶת עָשְׁרוֹ וּכְבוֹדוֹ?
לְךָ יֵשׁ שְׁנֵים-עָשָׂר בָּנִים וְלוֹ רַק שְׁנַיִם.
קַח אֶת בָּנֶיךָ לְחֶבְרוֹן וּקְבֹר אֶת אָבִיךְ.
עֲמֹד עַל יַד הַקֶּבֶר לִפְנֵי בְּנֵה
וְתִבַּע אֶת שֶׁלְּךָ.'

7.

'שִׁכְנְעוּ אוֹתִי לָשֵׂאת אִשָּׁה מִקְּרוֹבֵינוּ—
יָדַעְתִּי שֶׁבָּזוּ אֶת הַנָּשִׁים הַכְּנַעֲנִיוֹת שֶׁלִּי,
וְנִשְׁבַּעְתִּי שֶׁלֹּא אֶשָּׂא עוֹד בַּת מְקוֹמִית.
עָבַרְתִּי אֶת הַיַּבֹּק,
נִפְגַּשְׁתִּי עִם הַדּוֹד יִשְׁמָעֵאל,

Words for Blessing the World

arranged everything so that they would approve.
I didn't know that she wasn't the right kind of kin.
They didn't spell it out, at least not to me,
but Ya'akob always understood.
Esav, why don't you behave like Ya'akob,
learn to read and write like Ya'akob? Be
a good boy and follow the sheep, like Ya'akob."
I'll not be a sheep-follower,
not now, not
ever. I'm happy when I'm on my own, running down a deer
along the edge of the plain, carefully aiming my arrow,
shooting and striking its heart. I have brought them venison
many times, meat cooked with spices
from Uncle Ishmael. There will be plenty of spices
when I marry Basemat. And if they don't come to my feast,
I will curse them: May Ya'akob plant lentils behind your tent
that will fill your innards with wind."

8.
Why do you laugh, daughters of Lot?
Why do you stand with them, Tamar, mother of Judah's tribe?
"We stole seed from men; from fathers, we three gave birth to sons
and from their seed will come the anointed one, Messiah of Israel."

9.
"Do you remember, dear Nanny, when my father the king
asked impossible heroic deeds of him
and he returned, not with one hundred,
but with two hundred Philistine foreskins
to redden our marriage bed?

סִדַּרְתִּי אֶת הַכֹּל כְּדֵי שֶׁיַּסְכִּימוּ.
לֹא יָדַעְתִּי שֶׁהִיא לֹא הַקְּרוֹבָה הַנְּכוֹנָה.
לֹא אָמְרוּ בִּמְפֹרָשׁ, לְפָחוֹת לֹא לִי,
אֲבָל יַעֲקֹב תָּמִיד יָדַע.
עֵשָׂו, לָמָה לֹא תִּתְנַהֵג כְּמוֹ יַעֲקֹב,
לָמָה לֹא תִּקְרָא וְתִכְתֹּב כְּמוֹ יַעֲקֹב? תִּהְיֶה
יֶלֶד טוֹב וּתְעַקֵּב אַחֲרֵי הַצֹּאן כְּמוֹ יַעֲקֹב.
לֹא אֲעַקֵּב אַחֲרֵי צֹאן
לֹא עַכְשָׁו וְאַף פַּעַם
לֹא. אֶשְׂמַח כְּשֶׁאֲנִי לְבַד, רָץ אַחֲרֵי צְבִי
לְאֹרֶךְ קְצֵי הַמִּישׁוֹר, מְכַוֵּון חִיצִי בִּזְהִירוּת,
יוֹרֶה וּפוֹגֵעַ בְּלִבּוֹ. הֵבֵאתִי לָהֶם
בְּשַׂר צְבִי הַרְבֵּה פְּעָמִים, בָּשָׂר מְבֻשָּׁל בְּתַבְלִינִים
מֵהַדּוּד יִשְׁמָעֵאל. יִהְיוּ תַּבְלִינִים לָרֹב כְּשֶׁאֶתְחַתֵּן
עִם בָּשְׂמַת. אִם לֹא יָבוֹאוּ לַמִּשְׁתֶּה שֶׁלִּי,
אֲקַלֵּל אוֹתָם: שֶׁיַּעֲקֹב יִזְרַע עֲדָשִׁים מֵאַחֲרֵי אָהֳלֵיכֶם
שֶׁיִּמָּלְאוּ כְּלָיוֹתֵיכֶם בִּנְפִיחוֹת.'

8.

לָמָה אַתֶּן צוֹחֲקוֹת, בְּנוֹת לוֹט?
לָמָה אַתְּ עוֹמֶדֶת עִמָּן, תָּמָר, אֵם לְשֵׁבֶט יְהוּדָה?
'גָּזַלְנוּ זֶרַע מִגֶּבֶר; מֵאָבוֹת, שְׁלֹשְׁתֵּנוּ הוֹלַדְנוּ בָּנִים;
וּמִזַּרְעָם יָבוֹא מְשִׁיחַ יִשְׂרָאֵל.'

9.

'הִתְזַכְּרִי, אוֹמֶנֶת יְקָרָה, כְּשֶׁאָבִי הַמֶּלֶךְ
בִּקֵּשׁ מַעֲשֵׂי גְּבוּרָה בִּלְתִּי אֶפְשָׁרִיִּים מִמֶּנּוּ
וְהוּא שָׁב, לֹא עִם מֵאָה,
אֶלָּא עִם מָאתַיִם עָרְלוֹת פְּלִשְׁתִּים
לְהַאֲדִים אֶת מִשְׁכַּב חֲתֻנָּתֵנוּ?

Words for Blessing the World

Come to the window and see him now,
our David, our anointed one, our king
dancing and jumping like a monkey who shows
his bright red privates
to all the maidens of Jerusalem!"

10.
What did you learn from filling in the vacant spaces?
What did you gain from giving voice to the silences?
Have you found what was lost? What difference does it make
if you hear the voice of the oppressed
and don't change your life?
What do true poems matter
if master and slave still suffer,
ruled by the old stories?

בֹּאִי לַחַלּוֹן וּרְאִי אוֹתוֹ עַכְשָׁיו,
דָּוִד שֶׁלָּנוּ, מַלְכֵּנוּ, מְשִׁיחֵנוּ,
רוֹקֵד וְקוֹפֵץ כְּמוֹ קוֹף שֶׁמַּרְאֶה
אֶת מְבוּשָׁיו הָאֲדַמְדַּמִּים
לְכֹל בְּנוֹת יְרוּשָׁלַיִם!'

10.
מִמְּלוֹי הַחֲלָלִים, מַה לָּמַדְתָּ?
מַה הִרְוִוחַתְּ מִמַּתַּן קוֹל לַשְּׁתִיקוֹת?
הַמָצָאתָ מַה שֶּׁנֶּאֱבַד? מַה זֶה מְשַׁנֶּה
אִם אַתָּה שׁוֹמֵעַ אֶת קוֹל הַמְּדוּכָּאִים
וְלֹא מְשַׁנֶּה אֶת חַיֶּיךָ?
מַה מּוֹעִילָה שִׁירָה אֲמִיתִּית
אִם אָדוֹן וְעֶבֶד עֲדַיִן סוֹבְלִים
מִשִּׁלְטוֹן הַסִּפּוּרִים הַיְשָׁנִים?

I Believe with Perfect Faith

I believe with perfect faith
that the Jews came out of Egypt to testify
that there are narrow straits in every place
that all of us must pass through
to march toward a promised land
that we will not reach,
but which will never disappear from our eyes.

אֲנִי מַאֲמִין בֶּאֱמוּנָה שְׁלֵמָה

אֲנִי מַאֲמִין בֶּאֱמוּנָה שְׁלֵמָה
שֶׁהַיְהוּדִים יָצְאוּ מִמִּצְרַיִם לְהָעִיד
שֶׁיֵּשׁ מֵיצָרִים בְּכָל מָקוֹם
שֶׁכֻּלָּנוּ צְרִיכִים לַעֲבֹר כְּדֵי
לִצְעֹד לְאֶרֶץ מוּבְטַחַת
שֶׁאַף פַּעַם לֹא נַגִּיעַ אֵלֶיהָ
וְשֶׁלֹּא תֵּעָלֵם מֵעֵינֵינוּ לְעוֹלָם.

III

As Our Father Neared Death

As our father neared death, his mind raced
between fantasies and the facts of his life,
his speech like the black box of an airplane that had crashed,
the record of its journey jumbled beyond reconstruction.
My brother and I cared for him, sometimes
feeding, sometimes reading to him
from the Book of Psalms. I led him
beside green pastures and still waters
when, he, in a soft voice, as if from far away, blessed me:
May God bless you and keep you, May God shine His Face upon you,
until its end. Am I not the brother who wrapped himself in a tallit,
who stood before the congregation on Shabbat and holidays
to lead it in prayer to an improbable God? But all that ritual
razzmatazz fooled my fond old man and me.

After his death, my brother came every Shabbat and holiday
to say Kaddish with our mother.
She said to me every Sunday when I visited her,
"Your father would be so happy
that your brother is saying Kaddish for him."
Thus my brother received her blessing, for the great kindness
he did her, a kindness that only the living can receive.

כְּשֶׁאָבִינוּ גָּסַס

כְּשֶׁאָבִינוּ גָּסַס, מוֹחוֹ מִהֵר
בֵּין פַנְטַזְיוֹת וְעוּבְדוֹת חַיָּיו,
שְׂפָתוֹ כְּקוּפְסָה שְׁחוֹרָה שֶׁל מָטוֹס נִתְרַסֵּק
שֶׁהַקְלָטַת נְסִיעָתוֹ מְבוּלְבֶּלֶת לְלֹא שִׁחְזוּר.
אֲנִי וְאָחִי טִפַּלְנוּ בּוֹ, לִפְעָמִים
מַאֲכִילִים, לִפְעָמִים קוֹרְאִים לוֹ
מִסְפַּר תְּהִילִים. הֵנַחְתִּי אוֹתוֹ
לִנְאוֹת דֶּשֶׁא וּלְמֵי מְנוּחוֹת
וְהוּא, בְּקוֹל רַךְ, כְּאִילוּ מִמֶּרְחַקִּים, בֵּרַךְ אוֹתִי:
יְבָרֶכְךָ יי וְיִשְׁמְרֶךָ, יָאֵר יי פָּנָיו אֵלֶיךָ,
עַד סוֹפוֹ. הֲלֹא אֲנִי הָאָח שֶׁהִתְעַטֵּף בְּטַלִּית,
שֶׁעָמַד לִפְנֵי הַקָּהָל כִּשְׁלִיחוֹ בְּשַׁבָּת וּבְחַגִּים,
וְצִלְצוּלֵי הַצָּנְתִי שֶׁגָּעוּ גַּם אוֹתִי, גַּם אֶת אָבִי.

אַחֲרֵי מוֹתוֹ, אָחִי בָּא כָּל שַׁבָּת וְיוֹם טוֹב
לֹאמַר קַדִּישׁ עִם אָמֵנוּ.
כָּל יוֹם רִאשׁוֹן כְּשֶׁבִּקַּרְתִּי אוֹתָהּ, אָמְרָה לִי:
'אָבִיךָ כֹּה יִשְׂמַח
שֶׁאָחִיךָ אוֹמֵר קַדִּישׁ בִּשְׁבִילוֹ.'
כָּךְ אָחִי קִבֵּל בִּרְכָתָהּ, בִּגְלַל הַחֶסֶד הַגָּדוֹל שֶׁעָשָׂה
בִּשְׁבִילָהּ, חֶסֶד שֶׁרַק אֵלֶּה שֶׁחַיִּים מְקַבְּלִים.

Words for Blessing the World

To Yehuda Amichai

I said Kaddish when you died, a month
magnified and sanctified to give thanks for
the gift of your creations and to found
a new religion out of your sad and gentle wisdom.
You brought something new out of the terrible
Chad Gadya machine of Jewish history.
You gave us everyday psalms — of the builder
who cheated you, of the plums that you brought home
as an offering, of the lover who handed you
fresh towels each time you walked through her door.
Together, you became Bathsheba and David, conquering
the land with your love-making; every place you stripped off
your clothes — the caves at Nahal David,
the forests of Jerusalem, the beach at Caesarea — became witnesses
like Joshua's mounds at Gilgal. You remembered your wars,
yet you did not forget the peace when the man under his vine
will call up the man under his fig tree.
You commanded, "Thou shalt love"
and after fifty years of breaking the images of the God
you didn't believe in, you finally gave a name to your god:
"What has changed? Everything will change. Change is god
and death is its prophet."

You are our father, the father of our future.
May your name be made great and revered
amid god-wrestlers and life-lovers
everywhere and always.

לִיהוּדָה עֲמִיחַי

אָמַרְתִּי קַדִּישׁ אַחֲרֵי מוֹתְךָ, חֹדֶשׁ
שֶׁל יִתְגַּדַּל וְיִתְקַדַּשׁ לְהוֹדוֹת
עַל מַתְּנַת יְצִירוֹתֶיךָ וּלְיַסֵּד
דָּת חֲדָשָׁה מֵחָכְמָתְךָ הָעֲצוּבָה וְהָעֲדִינָה.
הוֹלַדְתָּ דָּבָר חָדָשׁ מִתְהַלֵּךְ מְכוֹנַת חַד גַּדְיָא
הָאֲיוּמָה שֶׁל תּוֹלְדוֹת הַיְּהוּדִים.
נָתַתָּ לָנוּ מִזְמוֹרִים יוֹם-יוֹמִיִּים — שֶׁל הַבַּנַאי
שֶׁרִימָה אוֹתְךָ, שֶׁל הַשְּׁזִיפִים שֶׁהֵבֵאתָ הַבַּיְתָה
כְּמַתָּנָה, שֶׁל הָאֲהוּבָה שֶׁהִגִּישָׁה
מַגֶּבֶת טְרִיּוֹת כָּל פַּעַם שֶׁבָּאתָ לְבֵיתָהּ.
בְּיַחַד, הֱיִיתֶם בַּת-שֶׁבַע וְדָוִד וְהִתְגַּבַּרְתֶּם
עַל הָאָרֶץ בְּדוֹדֵיכֶם; כָּל מָקוֹם שֶׁהִפְשַׁטְתֶּם
אֶת בִּגְדֵיכֶם — מְעָרוֹת נַחַל דָּוִד,
יְעָרוֹת יְרוּשָׁלַיִם, חוֹלוֹת קֵיסַרְיָא — הָיוּ לְעֵדִים
כְּגַלֵּי יְהוֹשֻׁעַ בַּגִּלְגָּל. זָכַרְתָּ מִלְחֲמוֹתֶיךָ,
וְלֹא שָׁכַחְתָּ אֶת הַשָּׁלוֹם, שֶׁאָז הָאִישׁ תַּחַת גַּפְנוֹ
יְטַלְפֵּן לָאִישׁ תַּחַת תְּאֵנָתוֹ.
צִוִּיתָ: תֹּאהֲבוּ
וְאַחֲרֵי חֲמִשִּׁים שָׁנִים שֶׁל שְׁבִירַת דְּמוּיוֹת הָאֱלֹהִים
שֶׁלֹּא הֶאֱמַנְתָּ בּוֹ, סוֹף-סוֹף נָתַתָּ שֵׁם לֵאלֹהֶיךָ:
'מַה נִּשְׁתַּנָּה? הַכֹּל יִשְׁתַּנֶּה. הַשִּׁנּוּי הוּא הָאֱלֹהִים
וְהַמָּוֶת נְבִיאוֹ.'

אַתָּה אָבִינוּ, אָב הֶעָתִיד שֶׁלָּנוּ.
יִתְגַּדַּל וְיִתְקַדַּשׁ שְׁמְךָ
בֵּין מִתְאַבְּקֵי אֱלוֹהַּ וְאוֹהֲבֵי חַיִּים
בְּכָל מָקוֹם תָּמִיד.

What I Received as an Inheritance

From my grandfather I inherited tefillin
and an old volume of Walt Whitman's Leaves of Grass.
Mornings, I put on his tefillin and read in his book,
"Why should I wish to see God more than this day?...
In the faces of men and women I see God
and in my own face in the mirror." Like him,
I know with every atom of my body
that all men and women are my holy brothers and sisters
and that my spirit is also tied to the plants in the field
and to the far stars.
Every time I read in his book, I come to know,
as did my unknown grandfather,
that I will follow this rebbe all the days of my life.

מַה שֶׁקִּבַּלְתִּי בִּירוּשָׁה

מִסָּבִי יָרַשְׁתִּי תְּפִילִין
וְכֶרֶךְ יָשָׁן שֶׁל עֲלֵי דֶשֶׁא מֵאֵת וַולְט וִויטְמַן
בַּבֹּקֶר אֲנִי מֵנִיחַ תְּפִילָיו וְקוֹרֵא בְּסִפְרוֹ,
'לָמָה אֲבַקֵּשׁ לִרְאוֹת אֱלוֹהַ יוֹתֵר מֵאֲשֶׁר יוֹם זֶה?...
אֶרְאֶה אֱלוֹהַ עַל פְּנֵי גְבָרִים וְנָשִׁים
וְעַל פְּנֵי בְּרָאִי.' כָּמוֹהוּ
יוֹדֵעַ אֲנִי עִם כָּל אָטוֹם בְּגוּפִי
שֶׁכָּל בְּנֵי אָדָם הֵם אַחַי וְאַחְיוֹתַי הַקְּדוֹשִׁים
וְשֶׁרוּחִי קְשׁוּרָה גַם לַצְּמָחִים בַּשָּׂדֶה
וְלַכּוֹכָבִים הָרְחוֹקִים.
כָּל פַּעַם שֶׁאֲנִי קוֹרֵא בְּסִפְרוֹ אֲנִי מִשְׁכְּנֵעַ
כְּמוֹ הַסָּב הַבִּלְתִּי יָדוּעַ שֶׁלִי,
שֶׁאֶעֱקֹב אַחֲרֵי הָרַבִּי הַזֶּה כָּל יְמֵי חַיַּי.

Words for Blessing the World

I Make a Covenant of Peace with You

I make a covenant of peace with you,
Reb Meshullam Zalman Schachter-Shalomi.
Thirty years I followed your lead;
I sought to bless and draw blessings from the universe
through the language of our ancient prayers.
I no longer can. To birth the future
like you I strike at the rock of the past.

אֲנִי כּוֹרֶתֶ בְּרִית שָׁלוֹם אִתָּךְ

אֲנִי כּוֹרֶתֶ בְּרִית שָׁלוֹם אִתָּךְ,
ר׳ מְשׁוּלָם זַלְמַן שַׁחְטֶר-שָׁלוֹמִי.
שְׁלֹשִׁים שָׁנָה עָקַבְתִּי אַחֲרֶיךָ;
נִסִּיתִי לְבָרֵךְ וְלִשְׁאֹב בְּרָכוֹת מִן הַיְּקוּם
בִּלְשׁוֹן תְּפִילוֹתֵינוּ הָעַתִּיקוֹת.
אֵינִי יָכוֹל עוֹד. לְהַחֲיוֹת אֶת הֶעָתִיד
כָּמוֹךָ אַכֶּה בְּאֶבֶן הֶעָבָר.

IV

Rebbe Nachman's Torah of the Void

Come and listen: In the beginning
there was only the light of God.
To make a world, God, may He be blessed, became compressed
(if a person dares to say such a thing)
and His light burst into fiery fragments,
millions on every side, dancing
in the void remaining after His self-compression.
His Spirit hovered over the face of the void,
which was no longer filled. A question:
does a trace of God remain in the void that God vacated?
Don't look for answers from the world
that doesn't believe in God. Look for answers
that arise like mist from the open void,
that come into being in silence, not in words,
and if silence doesn't satisfy you, then sing
what I taught you; the song without words
expresses the highest wisdom,
an endless tune for the wisdom without end,
which carries us over the open void
into the heart of compassion,
where our souls are filled
with the light hidden for the righteous,
the goal of life on this earthly plane
where we find ourselves.

תּוֹרַת הֶחָלָל לְרֶבִּי נַחְמָן

בֹּאוּ וְשִׁמְעוּ: בְּרֵאשִׁית
רַק אוֹר הָאֱלֹהִים נִמְצָא.
לִבְרֹא עוֹלָם, הוּא, יִתְבָּרַךְ, הִצְטַמְצֵם
(אִם בֶּן־אָדָם מֵעִיז לְאָמְרוֹ)
וְאוֹרוֹ הִתְפּוֹצֵץ לְשַׁבְרִירִים שׂוֹרְפִים,
מִילְיוֹנִים לְכָל צַד, מְרַקְּדִים
בֶּחָלָל שֶׁנִּשְׁאַר אַחֲרֵי הַצִּמְצוּם.
רוּחוֹ רָחֲפָה עַל פְּנֵי הֶחָלָל,
שֶׁעֲדַיִן לֹא נִמְלָא. שְׁאֵלָה:
הַאִם הָרֹשֶׁם שֶׁל אֱלֹהִים נִרְשַׁם בֶּחָלָל הַפָּנוּי
מִמֶּנּוּ? אַל תִּדְרְשׁוּ תְּשׁוּבוֹת מִן הָעוֹלָם
שֶׁלֹּא מַאֲמִין בֵּאלֹהִים. דִּרְשׁוּ תְּשׁוּבוֹת
שֶׁעוֹלוֹת כַּעֲרָפֶל מִן הֶחָלָל,
שֶׁמִּתְהַוּוֹת בִּדְמָמָה וְלֹא בְּמִילִים,
וְאִם דְּמָמָה לֹא תַסְפִּיק לָכֶם, תָּשִׁירוּ
מַה שֶּׁלִּמַּדְתִּי אֶתְכֶם; נִיגּוּן בְּלִי מִילִים
מְבַטֵּא אֶת הַחָכְמָה הָעֶלְיוֹנָה בְּיוֹתֵר,
נִיגּוּן בְּלִי סוֹף לְחָכְמָה אֵין־סוֹפִית,
שֶׁמַּשִּׂיא אוֹתָנוּ מֵעֵבֶר לֶחָלָל
לְלֵב הָרַחֲמָנוּת
שֶׁבּוֹ נִשְׁמוֹתֵינוּ מִתְמַלְּאוֹת
בָּאוֹר הַגָּנוּז לַצַּדִּיקִים,
תַּכְלִית חַיֵּינוּ בַּמַּדְרֵגָה הָאַרְצִית
שֶׁבָּהּ אָנוּ נִמְצָאִים.

A Song for Gratitude

What does it take to treasure each day,
to give thanks for the gifts not earned,
to savor the taste of every first fruit
and know that enough is as good as a feast?

It takes a lifetime to learn how to live,
to sort through the stuff that fills up our days,
to weigh and measure just what to claim
and know that enough is as good as a feast.

So sit at nightfall with those you love
and light a candle to greet the dark,
clasp hands as you bless the bread
and know that enough is as good as a feast.

Open your heart to the joy and the pain,
the bitter and sweet of the knowledge you've gained
and sweetly surrender to what you can't change
and know that enough is as good as a feast.

שִׁיר לְהוֹדָיָה

בַּמֶּה נִלְמַד לִטְמֹן כָּל יוֹם,
לְהוֹדוֹת עַל מַתָּנוֹת שֶׁלֹּא הִרְוַחְנוּ,
לִטְעֹם כָּל טַעַם שֶׁל פְּרִי חָדָשׁ,
לְגַלּוֹת שֶׁדַּי מַשְׂבִּיעַ כְּמוֹ מִשְׁתֶּה?

לִלְמֹד לִחְיוֹת צָרִיךְ חַיִּים אֲרוּכִּים:
לְמַיֵּין מַה שֶׁמְּמַלֵּא אֶת יָמֵינוּ,
לִשְׁקֹל וְלִמְדֹד מַה בְּדִיּוּק לִתְבֹּעַ
לְגַלּוֹת שֶׁדַּי מַשְׂבִּיעַ כְּמוֹ מִשְׁתֶּה.

שְׁבוּ בֵּין הָעַרְבַּיִים עִם אוֹהֲבִים
וְהַדְלִיקוּ נֵר לִפְנֵי הַחֹשֶׁךְ,
אֶחֱזוּ יָדַיִים לְבָרֵךְ עַל הַלֶּחֶם
לְגַלּוֹת שֶׁדַּי מַשְׂבִּיעַ כְּמוֹ מִשְׁתֶּה.

פִּתְחוּ לְבַבְכֶם לַשָּׂשׂוֹן וְלָעֶצֶב,
לַמַּר וְלַמָּתוֹק שֶׁהִשִּׂגְתֶּם בְּחָכְמָה
וְהִכָּנְעוּ בִּנְעִימוּת לְמַה שֶׁאֵין לְשַׁנּוֹת
לְגַלּוֹת שֶׁדַּי מַשְׂבִּיעַ כְּמוֹ מִשְׁתֶּה.

Author's Afterword   סוֹף דָּבָר

    Over thirty years ago, I spoke to my teacher, Rabbi Zalman Schachter-Shalomi, about my difficulty with the traditional language of Jewish prayer. Reb Zalman asked me if I thought I could say "you" to the universe. As he did to so many others, he gave me permission to experiment – in effect to use *barukh ata olam*, "blessed are you, world," as an inner mantra, even as he urged me to continue to recite the traditional words in prayer. It took me thirty years to realize that I needed to go further, to claim *barukh ata olam* as more than an inner mantra, by giving myself permission to say those words prayerfully. That discovery led to the creation of these prayerful poems.

    Through these poems, I hope to contribute to a reality-based, cosmos-centered approach to the world that is not limited by traditional Jewish narratives and rituals, but is nevertheless in an authentic relationship to them. It should be no surprise, therefore, that I have written them in both Hebrew and English, the two primary languages of the Jewish people in our time, one a world-language for a world-spanning people, and the other the traditional language of Jewish prayer, continuity and liturgical creativity. As a poet whose first language is English, I have found, nevertheless, that Hebrew is the home of my soul, the language in which I aspire to self-transcendence.

    This project of bi-lingual contemporary poems for the Jewish people was seeded by Shaul Magid's call in the 2015 Winter issue of Tikkun for forms of Jewish worship to embody Schachter-Shalomi's paradigm-changing approach to Jewish theology. In an accompanying sidebar approving Magid's message, Reb Zalman admitted that he had not been ready to initiate such a change during his life, but knew that its time was coming.

In his book *Paradigm Shift*, Schachter-Shalomi brought into Jewish discourse the Gaia hypothesis, formulated by biologists in the 1970s, which posits that biological organisms and the inorganic world form a unified, self-regulating system that preserves the conditions for continued life on Earth. Expressing this in evolutionary terms, humans are the embodiment of the cosmos becoming self-conscious, and, in moral terms, are therefore responsible for the future of that evolution. Gaia, Reb Zalman told us, was the living God, and we were Gaia's vanguard. These poems respond to the implication of that view that we need to look for religious inspiration to the holiness of the earth and all that is on it, rather than to any version of transcendence existing separate from us. From this cosmic vantage point, the categories in which Jews think about religion – God, Torah, Israel – Creation, Revelation, Redemption – look rather different and therefore need new a poetic language in which to be expressed. I hope that readers of this book will find it here.

At a visit I made to the National Museum of the American Indian, I made note of a remark made by the father of one the artists, Calvin Hunt of the Kwag'ul band, about the tradition of the Potlatch, the ceremony of mutual gift-giving and feasting between tribes: "If we did not carry on, our hearts would break." For many years, this was my rationale for accommodating myself to the theistic language of Jewish prayer. I said to myself, 'we inherited this tradition from our forebears at great cost to them. Who am I to throw it aside?' But increasingly, I have been saying to myself, 'If I carry on in this way, my mind will break.' I have written these bi-lingual, bi-cultural poems to bring heart and mind together. I will be very pleased if the poems do the same for others who may feel a similar need. And if any lines should find their way into the evolving liturgy of the Jewish people, so much the better.

*More poetry from
Ben Yehuda Press*

is

heretical Jewish blessings and poems

Yaakov Moshe

"The best mystical poets tell it like it really is. Funny, touching, sobering, and uplifting, the poems of Is remind us that we are an oh-so-ephemeral part of the cosmic nothing, barely glimpsing the nature of reality under our own skins. Yet these poems also remind us of our deepest experiences of being alive as individual embodied beings. Is invites us into stillness and emptiness, but also into laughter and love."
—**Rabbi Dr. Jill Hammer**, author of *The Hebrew Priestess*

"*is* is a very compelling book, full of Judaic Zen-like Koans and whispers that invite the reader to ponder what is, what isn't, and what might yet be."
—**Lesléa Newman**, author of *Heather Has Two Mommies* and *A Letter to Harvey Milk*

"These so-Jewish and so-Zennish poems are perfect prayers for the holy congregation of postmodern exiles, they who are eternally unsettled yet lovingly warmed by the flames of their unrequited yearning."
—**Avraham Leader**, founder of the Leader Minyan

Yaakov Moshe

if you have an idea of god
it is not god
god negates your idea
god is not anything you can think of except everything
god is not anywhere you can be except here
and when you are only here
you are not here

get quiet,
and consider one leaf:
the veins, the cells,
the exquisite complications,
photosynthesis,
intricate beyond any human invention;
and then it changes color,
and falls.

and consider
how many leaves are on a single tree,
and how many trees in a small patch of woods,
and how many woods in a forest,
and how many forests in a world.

get the picture?

Yaakov Moshe

My religion is not a matter of opinion
My religion is a matter of love

My spirituality does not depend on mythology
It requires only that you be moved by your myth

I don't care about the God you don't believe in
I want to know what prompts wonder in you
What form causes your mouth to gape
When are you so alive that you have only time for now
I want to know
when everything
for you
is here

I have more in common with the atheist who dances
Than with the so-called pious,
asleep.

So if you are sometimes in love with the world
then, sister, brother,
join me in this sweet caress
of the beloved
sometimes still and sometimes moving
sometimes loud and sometimes soft

If you are in love with this,
then you are the priests and priestesses
of my religion

"Sue Swartz does magnificent acrobatics with the Torah in *We Who Desire*. She takes the English that's become staid and boring, and adds something that's new and strange and exciting. These are poems that leave a taste in your mouth, and you walk away from them thinking, what did I just read? Oh, yeah. It's the Bible."
—Matthue Roth, author, *Yom Kippur A Go-Go, Never Mind the Goldbergs, My First Kafka*

Sue Swartz

This is the Instruction—

turn it & turn it // leave nothing out
the fire and the splendor
the fire   and the splendor

murmur and sigh
held in each white space

veiled prism of desire

your flesh and blood

We Who Desire

ENTROPY / FAITH

> *Abraham: Go forth from your native land and from your father's house to the land I will show you.*

We are nothing at first. Little more than dust, lucid
with possibility—
        Then fruit flies and feral dogs on our way
to becoming a different kind of multitude.

Go forth, we are commanded, and one by one we go
careening into an arrangement we barely understand,
leave our ancestral home to make our way, strangers
parading about in fancy suits of flesh.

We sacrifice our choicest herds, mark the bodies
of our young, yet nothing seems to make us right.
Like a bird we crash into windows.

Like an inflamed god we destroy our things.

To be fair, there is naiveté on every side. The first law
of the universe goes like this—
        Energy neither comes nor goes, just whirls
about, fools us into believing there's something new
under the sun.

The second? Live long enough in the closed system
of a promise and things will go wrong.

Stars will fall off the edge, solar plexus flicker,
kneecap spin off wildly. This is the truth the dead know:
        The meat on our bones is dodge & ruse,
        short-lived show to tempt our acceptance.

And we do again and again, sign on the dotted line.

Sue Swartz

Even as eternity rights itself & the skin of our lives
fails to outlast time. Still we invoke the third law, the favored,
the one we call perfection.

We Who Desire

ELEGY

His sons Isaac and Ishmael buried him—

Everything begot then begets its opposite:
nothing stays itself for very long.

It was time for Abraham to go, and for his sons—

>One sent out, hand pressed firmly on his back,
one led forward by deception luminous as the stars—

To bury him.

Oh, to be a fly on the wall at Machpelah as the grand patriarch is laid within.

Tell me. Which son would speak first of his restless consolations?

Which of his many little deaths?

Sue Swartz

We Who Desire

"Intimate and meditative, SHIVA MOON has the quality of prayer, yet it's also the journal of a harrowing year, filled with mourning, recollection, and a struggle for spiritual equilibrium. With her celebrated gifts for pictorial and lyrical language (leavened here with Hebrew terms), Maxine Silverman enters the darkness of her beloved father's death and seeks a way to accommodate his loss. Everything around her keeps changing: the moon, her garden, her children, even her absent father who grows more vivid with memory. The only constant is the momentous presence of God, glorious but silent. This is a wise, moving book for every reader—and a necessary book for anyone who's known loss."
—**Joan Murray**, author, *Swimming for the Ark*

Maxine Silverman

What I Learned So Far

When Ellen says my poems these days seem one seamless Kaddish,
I hear she understands the six months
before my father died were raw keen k'riah.

How June's visit home I see his death
forming in the air he breathes.

Why every evening I call him
until there's nothing left to say,
until all that remains—the sheer
pleasure of his company.

Elul. He weakens before my eyes,
no shofar blast required.

        Tishri. We daven
repetitions to dwell in meaning: who shall live
and who shall die, who in the fullness of years

        We cross into wilderness, a new year,
pillar of fire before us, the old, the weak, the infirm
to the rear, Amalek plucking them one death
at a time.

        Reservations for December.
My father says, "Come right now." and I do.

A way is made.
Gathered to his people,
a story old as time.

Shiva Moon

Putting the Garden to Bed

We live in different time zones, my sisters in Central,
I where the sun sets earlier the same sky.
There too, time flies.

The year rounds toward our father's yahrzeit.
In secular standard time and lunar,
we mark the days.

Putting the garden to bed for winter I think about borders
and beds blooming, their leaves taking in whatever light for days
and days on end, of plants feeding on light gathered
and stored in roots, tubers, corms and bulbs
until the whole earth is a squirrel with bulging cheeks.
At least this hemisphere.
On the other side earth ripens, lush, voluptuous
ovary opening purple, scarlet, gold, for every pollinator around,
clamoring unabashed and brazen, Take me
oh take me to your table your bodouir to your breast.

Wind picks up, the afternoon darkening.
Hurry. Mulch around the summer sweet,
smooth the cover of oak leaves where crocus and iris
will resume their habit of blooming.
Hands growing numb and still there's burning bush
and budelia . . . Sedalia, where he lies buried–

you name it–maples in fall, apples in spring, tomatoes
in summer, Juicy Fruit offered to some kid, the way my son holds
his fork,
evening light and morning's, a particular phase of the moon,
certain acts of kindness–
anything at all might bring him to mind.

Maxine Silverman

Right now I happen to be putting the garden to bed,
watering the shrubs, coiling the hose, going in to call my sisters,
Remember how   and   *Remember the time,*
what passes for hope among bare branches,
cold comfort in other words.

Shiva Moon

We Dream of a Green Rowboat, Amber Lake

As a boy her father rowed across the lake for mail,
    to Bud & Bailey's for eggs, news, and milk.
Across the lake she sees his childhood home
    and hers, behind it oak, maple, sumac ascending,
rise after brilliant rise to the tree line, a mountain's way
    of saying *where the air thins only memory of trees*
and the wish for trees grow.

    At first his shoulders burned a little rowing back,
then the oars' dip and pull were no more work than breathing.
    The oar locks' scrape reminds her a little of geese aunking,
the flare of oars their wings rising over the lake, her arms aching,
    of stories her father told when she was young. So she keeps
on rowing, rows and rows as if her life depends on rowing,
    a green rowboat, eggs and milk.

Maxine Silverman

www.ingramcontent.com/pod-product-compliance
Lightning Source LLC
LaVergne TN
LVHW041345080426
835512LV00006B/618